SCIENCE TIMELINES

THE ADVENT OF ELECTRICITY

1800 - 1900

By Charlie Samuels

W
FRANKLIN WATTS
LONDON · SYDNEY

First published in Great Britain in 2015 by
The Watts Publishing Group

Copyright © 2015 Brown Bear Books Ltd

For Brown Bear Books Ltd:
Editorial Director: Lindsey Lowe
Managing Editor: Tim Cooke
Children's Publisher: Anne O'Daly
Design Manager: David Poole
Designer: Kim Browne
Picture Manager: Sophie Mortimer
Production Director: Alastair Gourlay

Dewey no. 509

ISBN: 978 1 4451 4255 5

Printed in China

Franklin Watts
An imprint of
Hachette Children's Group
Part of the Watts Publishing Group
Carmelite House
50 Victoria Embankment
London EC4Y 0DZ

An Hachette UK company
www.hachette.co.uk

www.franklinwatts.co.uk

Contents

Introduction

The 19th century marked many scientific turning points. By its end, scientists had worked out the answers to problems that could still only be guessed at in 1800.

Where do humans come from? How do organisms inherit qualities from their parents? How old is the Earth? What are the building blocks of substances? How does disease spread? What is the nature of electricity? By 1900, researchers had come up with answers to such questions that are still largely accepted today. Many of the individual scientists were enthusiastic amateurs, as in earlier decades. By the end of the century, however, science was increasingly a specialised pursuit followed in laboratories by academics who were effectively professional scientists.

Theory and Practice

Many of the developments covered in this book were theoretical. People made careful observations and studies and then came up with a theory to explain them. Charles Darwin's theory of evolution, Gregor Mendel's theory of genetics and Dmitri Mendeleyev's theories about the nature of elements could only be proved later, when scientific knowledge caught up with their insights. Other developments were practical, however, and few were as influential as the invention of the internal combustion engine, which would begin a transport revolution that would lead to the coming not only of the age of the motor car but also of the aeroplane.

About This Book

This book uses timelines to describe scientific and technological advances from about 1800 to about 1900. A continuous timeline of the period runs along the bottom of all the pages. Its entries are colour-coded to indicate the different fields of science to which they belong. Each chapter also has a subject timeline, which runs vertically down the side of the page.

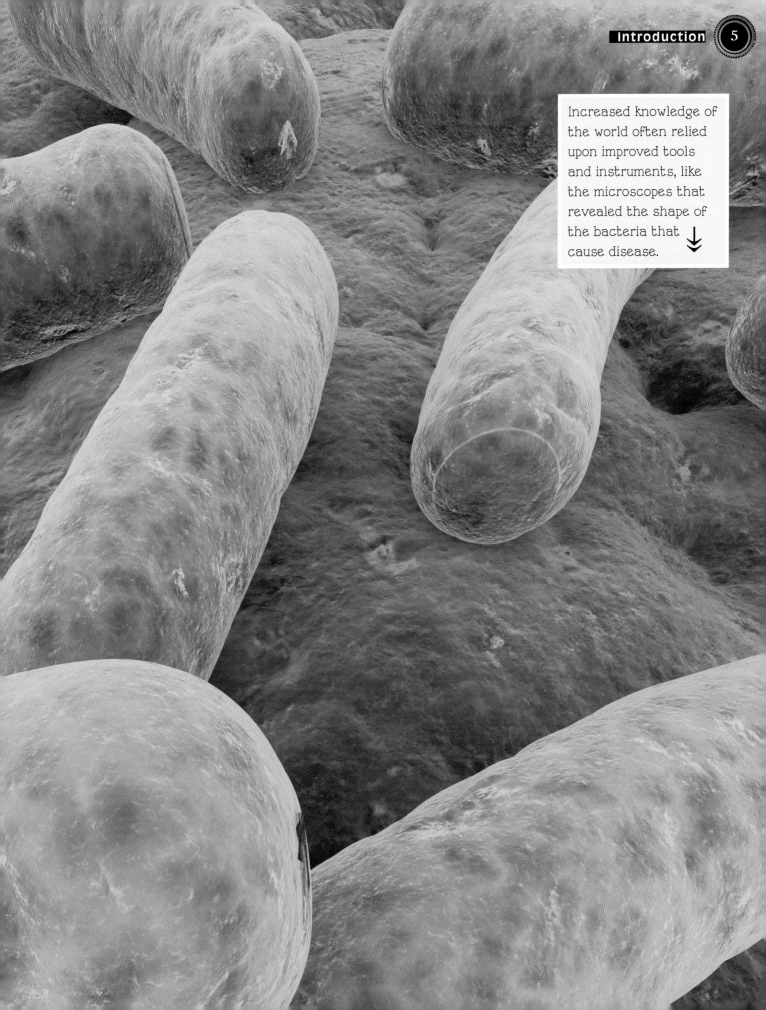

Increased knowledge of the world often relied upon improved tools and instruments, like the microscopes that revealed the shape of the bacteria that cause disease. ↓

Evidence in Fossils

Fossils are the remains of plants and animals that have been dead for a very long time. They are usually the hard parts of animals that have been changed to rock.

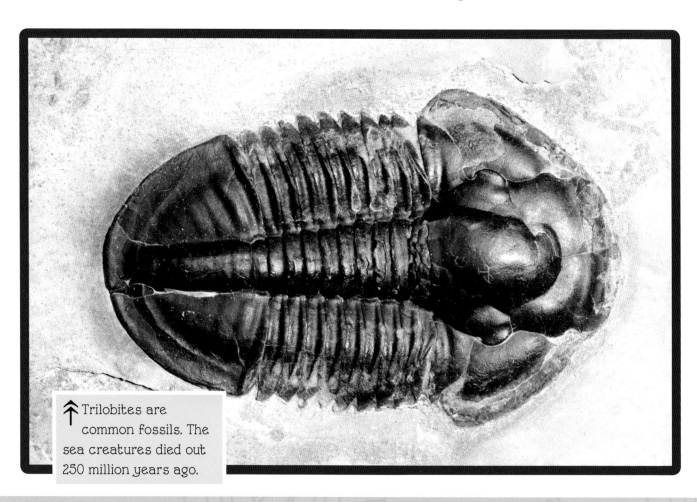

↑ Trilobites are common fossils. The sea creatures died out 250 million years ago.

TIMELINE 1800–1805

KEY:
- Astronomy and Maths
- Chemistry and Physics
- Biology and Medicine
- Inventions and Engineering

1800 English astronomer William Herschel discovers infrared radiation (from the Sun).

1801 English physicist Thomas Young observes the interference of light.

1802 French naturalist Jean-Baptiste Lamarck introduces the word 'biology' for the study of living things and life processes.

1800

1801

1802

1800 Italian astronomer Giuseppe Piazzi locates Ceres, the first asteroid (minor planet) to be discovered.

1800 Italian physicist Alessandro Volta invents the voltaic pile battery for producing a continuous electric current.

↑ Mary Anning became one of the most successful 19th-century fossil hunters.

In 1517, the Italian physician and poet Girolamo Fracastoro was probably the first person to suggest that fossils are the remains of living organisms. But no one took much notice at the time, and it was not until the fossil finds in Europe of the late 18th century that scientists began to realise that fossils can tell us a great deal about the history of living things and the rocks in which they are found.

In 1793, French naturalist Jean-Baptiste Lamarck (1744–1829) revived the idea that fossils represent ancient organisms, and this time other scientists began to listen to the argument. Two years later, another Frenchman, Georges Cuvier (1769–1832), discovered one of the first dinosaur fossils, although the word 'dinosaur', which comes from Greek words meaning 'terrible lizard', only came later when the famous British fossil hunter Richard Owen (1804–1892) invented the term in 1842.

Timeline

1517 Fracastoro suggests fossils are animal remains

1793 Lamarck revives Fracastoro's theory

1795 Cuvier discovers a dinosaur fossil

1811 Mary Anning discovers an ichthyosaur fossil

1816 William Smith proposes fossil–rock date correlation

↑ These are ancient dinosaur bones preserved in stone.

1803 English chemist John Dalton proposes his atomic theory: that elements are made up of indivisible atoms that combine to form chemical compounds.

1804 English inventor and founder of the science of aerodynamics George Cayley builds and flies a model glider.

1803

1804

1805

1803 English engineer Richard Trevithick makes the first steam-powered railway locomotive.

1803 German physician John Otto describes the inherited blood disorder haemophilia.

1805 French inventor Joseph Jacquard constructs a loom that is controlled by a 'chain' of punched cards.

Mary Anning, Fossil Hunter

As sea cliffs become eroded by waves and weather, sedimentary rocks release any fossils they contain. In 1811, schoolgirl Mary Anning was walking on a beach in Dorset, southern England, when she found a complete fossil skeleton of an ichthyosaur, a fish-like reptile that swam in the seas 150 million years ago during the Mesozoic Era. The enterprising 12-year-old sold her find to a museum and went on to become one of the world's best-known fossil collectors.

How Fossils Form

Palaeontologists (scientists who study fossils) discovered several ways in which fossils can form. Animal remains need to be buried quickly, before the carcass can decay or be eaten by scavengers. The best place for that to happen is under water, in the mud or sediment at the bottom of a lake or sea. That is also the place where sedimentary rocks form. Remains embedded in sediment may be dissolved by water, leaving behind a perfect mould. Minerals may be deposited in the mould, forming a cast often made from a totally different type of rock from the sediment. Footprints or animal tracks in mud can be preserved in a similar way. Preserving a whole animal only happens occasionally when conditions are right, as when insects become trapped in amber (fossilised tree resin) or mammoths are buried in the permanently frozen ground of the permafrost. Sometimes, even human skeletons have been fossilised. Tar pits in California have preserved some complete skeletons of prehistoric animals.

TIMELINE
1805–1810

KEY:
- Astronomy and Maths
- Chemistry and Physics
- Biology and Medicine
- Inventions and Engineering

1805 French naturalist Georges Cuvier founds the science of comparative anatomy.

1806 French chemists identify the first amino acid, asparagine (in asparagus).

1807 US engineer Robert Fulton builds a successful paddle steamer, *Clermont*.

1805

1806

1807

1805 English naval officer Francis Beaufort devises the Beaufort scale for classifying the strength of winds.

1806 Swiss mathematician Jean-Robert Argand devises the Argand diagram for representing complex numbers as points on a coordinate plane.

1807 The Royal Geological Society is founded in London.

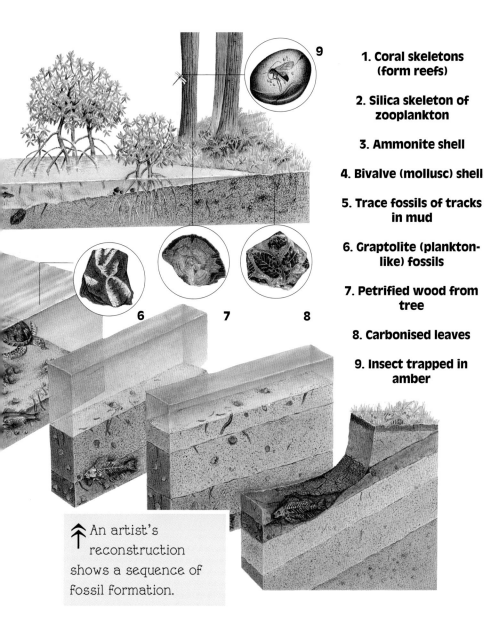

1. Coral skeletons (form reefs)

2. Silica skeleton of zooplankton

3. Ammonite shell

4. Bivalve (mollusc) shell

5. Trace fossils of tracks in mud

6. Graptolite (plankton-like) fossils

7. Petrified wood from tree

8. Carbonised leaves

9. Insect trapped in amber

⬆ An artist's reconstruction shows a sequence of fossil formation.

Using Fossils for Dating

Over millions of years, sedimentary rocks form strata (layers) one above the other. As long as no great upheavals disturb them, younger rock layers always lie on top of older ones. In 1816, geologist William Smith showed that the age of a fossil must be the same as that of the rock in which it is found. This provided a new method of geological dating. Absolute dating of fossils had to await 20th-century techniques such as radiocarbon dating.

1808 English chemist Humphry Davy invents the arc lamp.

1809 French naturalist Jean-Baptiste Lamarck proposes the (now discredited) theory that acquired characteristics, such as a weightlifter's muscles, are passed on from parents to their offspring.

1808

1809

1810

1808 French physicist Siméon Poisson puts forward a theory to account for irregularities in the orbits of the planets.

1808 English inventor George Cayley builds an unmanned glider.

1810 French chef Nicolas Appert invents food canning (originally for Napoleon's army).

The Birth of Photography

The camera had its beginnings nearly 1,000 years before film, which had to await the discovery of light-sensitive chemicals that could 'capture' the camera's image.

⟫ In 1843, William Fox Talbot set up a photographic 'factory' in his greenhouse.

TIMELINE
1810–1815

1811 English astronomer William Herschel proposes a theory that stars develop from nebulae as clouds of gas condense into star clusters.

1811 Italian scientist Amedeo Avogadro proposes Avogadro's law: that at the same temperature and pressure, equal volumes of all gases contain the same number of molecules.

1810   1811   1812

KEY:
- Astronomy and Maths
- Chemistry and Physics
- Biology and Medicine
- Inventions and Engineering

1810 German engineer Friedrich König invents a steam-powered printing press.

1811 Schoolgirl Mary Anning discovers the first fossil of an ichthyosaur in southern England.

The origin of the camera was the camera obscura (Latin for 'dark chamber'), a windowless room with a small hole in one wall. Light entering the hole forms an upside-down image of the scene outside on the opposite wall. Artists used the device as an aid to trace an image, and later it became portable in the form of a large light-excluding box. In this version, a glass lens soon replaced the hole.

↑ Early cameras were clumsy to use; they had to be large to hold photographic plates.

Fixing an Image on Paper

In 1725, the German physician Johann Schulze found that certain silver salts turn dark when exposed to daylight. Fifty years later, Swedish chemist Karl Scheele discovered that the darkening effect is due to the presence of grains of metallic silver. As a result, silver salts were to become standard ingredients in photographic emulsions (light-sensitive coatings) for films, paper and even leather – as tried in the late 1790s by Englishman Thomas Wedgwood.

Timeline

1725 Light sensitivity of silver salts is discovered

1826 Niépce takes his first successful photograph

1839 Louis Daguerre introduces daguerreotypes

1851 The wet-collodion process is introduced

1888 The first Kodak camera goes on sale

↑ An artist uses a camera obscura to re-create an outdoor scene indoors.

1813 Swiss botanist Augustin de Candolle devises a plant classification system, which he calls a 'taxonomy'.

1814 German physicist Joseph von Fraunhofer invents the spectroscope.

1813

1814

1815

1813 English engineer William Hedley builds his steam locomotive *Puffing Billy*.

1814 Spanish-born physician Matthieu Orfila founds the modern science of toxicology, the study of poisons.

1815 French physicist Augustin-Jean Fresnel discovers the diffraction (bending) of light as it passes through a small opening.

How a Camera Obscura Works

In a portable camera obscura, a lens focuses light from a scene onto a mirror. The mirror, angled at 45 degrees, reflects the image upwards onto a glass screen. An artist can then trace the image. This method may have been used by the painter Canaletto, who made detailed cityscapes. The camera obscura was used as an artist's aid until it was replaced by photographs after the 1850s.

→→ The portable camera obscura was a box fitted with a lens and a mirror.

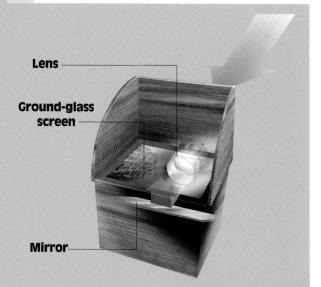

Lens

Ground-glass screen

Mirror

In France, Joseph Niépce experimented with fleeting silver images. His first successful photograph in 1826 used a polished pewter (metal) plate coated with bitumen (tar) as the light-sensitive substance.

In 1839, Frenchman Louis Daguerre used iodine to make photographic plates. He exposed the plate in a camera and 'developed' it in mercury vapour. The image was made permanent, or 'fixed', in a solution of common salt. These daguerreotypes, as his images were known, were mirror images and were used only once.

A Series of Improvements

In 1841, English chemist William Fox Talbot patented his calotype process. After exposure to light in a camera, the film was developed in a solution of gallic acid and fixed. The resulting 'negative' image (with black and white reversed) was placed with a sheet of light-sensitive paper and changed back to positive. This stage could be repeated many times.

TIMELINE
1815–1820

1815 English geologist William Smith publishes a geological map of the rocks of England and Wales.

1815 In England, chemist Humphry Davy and engineer George Stephenson independently invent a safety lamp for miners.

KEY:

- Astronomy and Maths
- Chemistry and Physics
- Biology and Medicine
- Inventions and Engineering

1815   1816   1817

1815 English scholar Peter Roget devises a slide rule with two logarithmic scales to help with multiplication and division.

1816 Scottish engineer Robert Stirling invents a two-cylinder external combustion engine.

1817 French chemists discover chlorophyll, the light-absorbing pigment in plants.

Fox Talbot established himself as one of the world's first professional photographers, with a studio in Reading, southern England, where the rich and famous had their portraits taken between 1843 and 1847. The texture of the paper meant the prints remained slightly coarse. Frenchman Louis-Désiré Blanquart-Evrard made more improvements in 1850 by coating the printing paper with albumen (egg white).

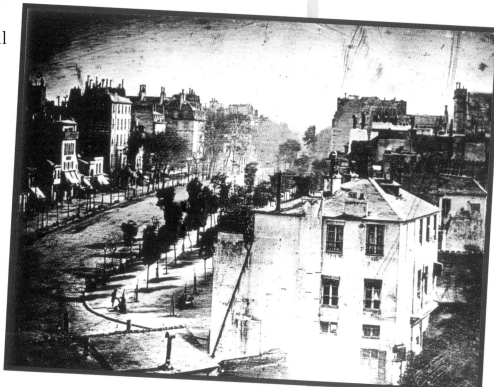

↑ This daguerreotype of a street in Paris, made by Daguerre in 1839, is the first-ever photograph to include a human being.

A Londoner, Frederick Archer, invented the wet-collodion process in 1851. It was used until dry plates, using gelatine emulsions, superseded it in the late 1870s. American George Eastman used a dry gelatine emulsion for his first Kodak camera of 1888, initially on paper film and a year later on transparent celluloid. With the Kodak, the era of mass-market photography had arrived.

1818 German-born English engineer Rudolph Ackermann devises a steering mechanism for horse-drawn carriages; it remains the basis of steering in modern cars.

1819 British astronomer John Herschel discovers that sodium thiosulphate can 'fix' a newly developed photographic image.

1820 The Royal Astronomical Society is founded in London.

1818 1819 1820

1819 US engineers Stephen McCormick and Jethro Wood independently produce a cast-iron plough.

1819 German inventor Augustus Siebe develops a pressurised diving suit, complete with helmet.

Michael Faraday

Faraday was a physicist and a chemist, one of the greatest experimental scientists who ever lived. He founded the sciences of electromagnetism and electrochemistry.

⟶⟩ Faraday's Christmas lectures presented science in a simple way to non-scientific audiences.

TIMELINE 1820–1825

KEY:
- Astronomy and Maths
- Chemistry and Physics
- Biology and Medicine
- Inventions and Engineering

1820 Danish physicist Hans Ørsted discovers electromagnetism when he notices the needle of a compass is deflected by an electric current.

1821 French astronomer Alexis Bouvard observes irregularities in the orbit of the planet Uranus; they prove to be caused by the gravity of Neptune.

1822 Charles Babbage makes a mechanical adding machine, or 'difference engine'.

1820

1821

1822

1820 French chemists discover the alkaloid quinine, soon to be used to treat malaria.

1821 US engineer Zachariah Allen installs the first hot-air central heating system.

1822 French naturalist Jean-Baptiste Lamarck distinguishes between vertebrates and invertebrates.

Michael Faraday, the son of a blacksmith, was born just outside London. At 13, he left school to become an apprentice bookbinder. Reading some of the books stirred his interest in science. He even carried out simple experiments with electricity. In 1813, he became assistant to English chemist Humphry Davy at the Royal Institution, where part of his job was to set up experiments for Davy's lectures. In 1827, he took over Davy's post of lecturer at the Royal Institution, becoming professor of chemistry there in 1833.

Chemical Discoveries

Faraday made several discoveries in chemistry. In 1823, he liquefied the gas chlorine by heating it in a sealed tube; previously only two other gases had been liquefied. In 1825, Faraday discovered benzene. In 1834, he turned his attention to electrolysis, the process in which an electric current passing through a solution (electrolyte) between two electrodes brings about chemical change. A gas is

Timeline

1821 Faraday makes the first simple electric motor

1823 Faraday makes liquid chlorine

1825 He discovers benzene

1831 He discovers electromagnetic induction and makes a simple dynamo

1834 Faraday writes his laws of electrolysis

← Michael Faraday is shown here in his role as a chemist. His most important discovery was that of benzene, the first of the so-called aromatic hydrocarbons and the basis of a new branch of organic chemistry.

1823 Scottish chemist Charles Macintosh patents waterproof fabric made by impregnating cloth with rubber.

1824 French physicist Dominique Arago discovers magnetic induction – the production of an electric field by a changing magnetic field.

1823   1824   1825

1823 The medical journal *The Lancet* is published for the first time in London.

1824 Swedish chemist Jöns Berzelius discovers silicon; a year later Danish physicist Hans Ørsted prepares an impure form of aluminium.

1825 The Stockton and Darlington Railway, the first public steam railway, opens in northern England.

Magnetic Fields

Surrounding every magnet is a field of force known as a magnetic field. Faraday studied the interaction between such fields and electric currents flowing in wires and other conductors. This branch of physics is now called electromagnetism. It is the basis of most electrical machines, from motors and dynamos to the electric bell, the relay and the solenoid (a type of electric switch).

⟫ The angle of the coil dictates whether or not a magnetic field produces a turning force (top) or not (below).

produced at either electrode, or a metal is deposited on the negatively charged cathode. The experiments led to Faraday's laws of electrolysis: 1. The amount of chemical change is proportional to the quantity of electricity; 2. The amount of change (produced by a fixed quantity of electricity) in different substances is proportional to the equivalent weight of the substance.

The Electric Motor

In physics, Faraday made the first primitive electric motor in 1821. He suspended a length of stiff wire next to a bar magnet that projected vertically from a dish of mercury. When he connected a battery between the mercury and the top of the wire, the lower end of the

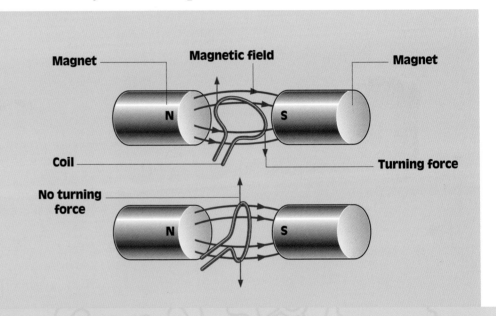

TIMELINE
1825–1830

KEY:

Astronomy and Maths

Chemistry and Physics

Biology and Medicine

Inventions and Engineering

1825

1826

1827

1825 French naturalist Georges Cuvier puts forward his catastrophe theory of extinction, that cataclysmic events cause species to become extinct.

1826 French chemist Joseph Niépce takes the first photograph (on a metal plate).

1827 US artist John James Audubon publishes the first part of *Birds of America*.

1825 English chemist and physicist Michael Faraday discovers benzene and several of its compounds.

1826 German astronomer Heinrich Olbers puts forward his famous paradox: why is the sky dark at night when the universe is full of stars?

wire rotated around the magnet. In 1831, Faraday wound two separate coils of wire around an iron ring. He connected one wire to a galvanometer (an instrument that detects an electric current). When he connected a battery to the other wire, the galvanometer needle registered a current. He also showed that when a magnet is moved in and out of a wire coil, a current is generated in the coil. Faraday had discovered the phenomenon of electromagnetic induction.

Faraday made many lasting contributions, including the children's Christmas lectures, which he started at the Royal Institution in 1826 and which he continued for 19 years. His 'The Chemical History of a Candle' is still published, and eminent scientists still give the lectures. Faraday's name is commemorated in two scientific units. The farad is the SI unit of capacitance, and the Faraday constant is the electric charge carried by 1 mole of electrons or singly charged ions.

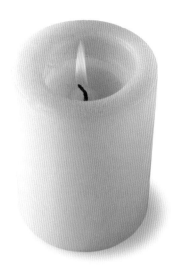

↑ The candle was the subject of one of Faraday's most popular lectures.

The Principle of the Electric Motor

Faraday demonstrated the principle of the electric motor with this simple apparatus. A copper rod, pivoted at the top, dips into a pool of mercury alongside a vertical magnet. When a current flows along the rod, the rod rotates around the magnet.

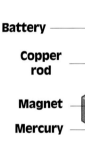

Battery
Copper rod
Magnet
Mercury

1828 French physiologist Pierre Flourens explains how the semicircular canals in the inner ear control the sense of balance.

1829 Blind French teacher Louis Braille invents the Braille alphabet to allow blind people to read.

1828   1829   1830

1828 Estonian naturalist Karl von Baer founds the science of embryology.

1829 George Stephenson's *Rocket* locomotive wins trials to provide the power for the Liverpool & Manchester Railway.

1830 US engineer Peter Cooper builds *Tom Thumb*, the first locomotive to be made in North America.

Darwin and Evolution

In 1831, Charles Darwin set sail on HMS *Beagle*. During his voyage, the observations he made eventually led to his theory of evolution through natural selection.

← Darwin plays with a monkey companion in this cartoon. Darwin's idea that humans were descended from apes was widely mocked in popular magazines.

TIMELINE
1830–1835

1830 Scottish writer Mary Somerville publishes a book of popular astronomy, *The Mechanism of the Heavens*.

1831 English scientist Michael Faraday makes a simple dynamo.

1832 French chemist Pierre Robiquet discovers codeine (in opium from poppies).

1830 Scottish chemist Andrew Ure invents the bimetallic strip thermostat.

1831 English naval officer James Ross locates the position of the magnetic north pole (which constantly changes).

1830   1831   1832

KEY:

Astronomy and Maths

Chemistry and Physics

Biology and Medicine

Inventions and Engineering

Charles Darwin (1809–1882), grandson of English physician Erasmus Darwin, was 22 years old when he joined HMS *Beagle*. The young man's duty was to provide company for the ship's captain, because the conventions of the time did not allow the captain to socialise with his officers or crew.

Darwin wanted to be a naturalist, and he used the five-year voyage to study plants and animals in faraway places. The ship visited islands off the west coast of Africa before sailing around Cape Horn and up the western coast of South America. It then stopped in the Galápagos Islands before sailing across the Pacific to Tahiti and New Zealand. It headed back to England by way of Mauritius and South Africa. At each stop, Darwin went ashore to observe local flora and fauna and collect specimens of rocks, plants and animals.

Observing the Animals

In South America, Darwin spent much of his time ashore. He studied the rocks and geology of the places he visited. In Patagonia, he found a shore with a 6-metre-high (20-foot) cliff containing some huge bones. They were too large to belong to any living creature. He observed that – apart from size – the bones resembled those of South American armadillos and sloths. He realised that their giant ancestors had become extinct, but why? Were they not suitable to survive?

Timeline

1831–1836 Voyage of HMS *Beagle*

1838 Darwin reads *An Essay on the Principle of Population* by Thomas Malthus

1858 He writes a joint paper with Alfred Russel Wallace

1859 He publishes *On the Origin of Species*

Isla Pinta (Abingdon)
Isla Genovesa (Tower)
Isla Marchena (Bindloe)
Equator
Isla San Salvador (James)
Isla Fernandina (Narborough)
Isla Isabela (Albermarle)
Isla Santa Cruz (Indefatigable)
Isla San Cristóbal (Chatham)
Galápagos Islands
Isla Santa María (Charles)
Isla Española (Hood)

↑ The Galápagos Islands provided Darwin with much evidence for evolution.

1833 English mathematician Charles Babbage begins work on his 'analytical engine', a type of mechanical computer (which he never finishes).

1834 English scientist Michael Faraday formulates the laws of electrolysis.

1833

1834

1835

1833 US engineer Obed Hussey invents a reaping machine.

1833 US Army surgeon William Beaumont explains the role of gastric juices in digestion.

1834 US engineer Cyrus McCormick patents a reaping and binding machine, an early form of combine harvester.

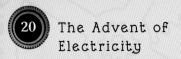

The Finches of the Galápagos Islands

In the Galápagos, Darwin found species of finches that differed only in coloration and the shapes of their beaks. The finches that ate seeds had short, stubby beaks, while birds that ate insects had long, thin beaks. Darwin deduced that they were variations of a species that had gradually evolved beaks appropriate to their chosen food.

→→ Finches 1, 3 and 4 have long beaks for eating insects; finch 2 is a fruit-eating species; and the beaks of finches 5 and 6 are best for tackling seeds.

The *Beagle* returned to England in October 1836, and Darwin moved to London. He studied geology and was converted to the ideas of geologist Charles Lyell, who argued that Earth was in a constant state of change.

Forming a Theory

Darwin's main concern was animal species: what happens if species produce many offspring when there is insufficient food for all of them? Darwin's idea was that only the fittest animals survive, and that they did so because a process he called natural selection was taking place. 'Nature' – that is, an individual's strength or adaptability – decided which animals survived.

At the same time Darwin was at work, Welsh naturalist Alfred Russel Wallace came to similar conclusions based on his observations of Asian and Australasian animals. He wrote about his theories in 1858 and sent them to Darwin. The pair consulted and issued a joint paper.

In 1859, Darwin published his epic *On the Origin of Species*

TIMELINE
1835–1840

KEY:

- Astronomy and Maths
- Chemistry and Physics
- Biology and Medicine
- Inventions and Engineering

1835 1836 1837

1835 US manufacturer Samuel Colt produces a revolver with interchangeable parts.

1836 US engineer Thomas Davenport makes a model tram.

1836 Swedish chemist Jöns Berzelius discovers catalysts, which speed up chemical reactions.

1835 English photographer William Fox Talbot invents the calotype process, which produces paper negatives from which multiple photographic prints can be made.

1836 English naturalist Charles Darwin completes his voyage on HMS *Beagle*.

1837 US industrialist John Deere invents a steel plough.

↑ The Galápagos were so remote that species had evolved there in isolation.

by Means of Natural Selection. He argued that evolution takes place in stages by chance mutations. Favourable mutations are inherited and passed on to offspring to produce a gradual change in a whole species. Eventually new, fitter species come into existence and old, less fit ones become extinct.

Darwin and his contemporaries had no idea exactly how mutations take place. Unknown to them, heredity was being studied in an Austrian monastery by the monk Gregor Mendel. He grew generations of pea plants to figure out the basic laws of heredity – how offspring receive sets of inherited 'factors' that we now call genes. Genetics provides the means by which evolution takes place.

Darwin's Ideas and Human Society

Some thinkers tried to apply Darwin's theory of 'the survival of the fittest' to human society. This theory, or Social Darwinism, argued that it was right that some people – the 'fittest' – became successful while others remained poor. The theory was popular for a time, as it seemed to explain the wide differences between individuals' success and wealth. It was later rejected in favour of a more inclusive view, in which the rich help support the poor.

1838 French chemist Anselme Payen identifies cellulose, the basic material of all plants.

1839 US inventor Charles Goodyear develops a process to harden rubber.

1838   1839   1840

1838 US inventor Samuel Morse demonstrates his electric telegraph and the Morse code that it uses.

1839 French chemist Louis Daguerre invents the daguerreotype, a type of photograph taken on metal plates.

1839 German biologist Theodor Schwann suggests that all living matter is made up of cells.

Mendel and Genetics

Today, genetics is one of the major scientific disciplines.
But it had humble beginnings in an Austrian monastery
garden where Gregor Mendel grew pea plants.

←← Genetics would
eventually explain why
family members look like
one another.

TIMELINE
1840–1845

KEY:

Astronomy
and Maths

Chemistry
and Physics

Biology and
Medicine

Inventions and
Engineering

1840 German pathologist Jacob
Henle puts forward his germ theory
of disease: that infection is caused by
parasitic organisms invading the body.

1842 German physicist Julius von Mayer
states the principle of the conservation
of energy (that energy can be neither
created nor destroyed, merely changed
from one form to another).

1840   1841   1842

1840 German chemist
Christian Schönbein
discovers and names ozone.

1841 English engineer Joseph
Whitworth introduces a system
of standard screw threads.

1842 US surgeon
Crawford Long uses
ether as an anaesthetic.

Gregor Mendel (1822–1884) was born in Austrian Silesia (now the Czech Republic). He studied at college before becoming an Augustinian monk in 1843. He became interested in hybrids – plants grown by crossing two different species – and began to breed pea plants in 1856. Over the next six years he grew 30,000 plants, which he fertilised artificially by transferring pollen from one plant to another. For example, he crossed tall plants with short plants. He then counted the number of tall and short plants in the next and later generations. He found that all first-generation plants were tall, but the second generation had tall plants and short plants in the ratio of 3 to 1.

Factors of Inheritance

Mendel concluded that every plant receives two 'factors' of inheritance, one from each parent. In the first generation of peas in the example, each plant receives a factor for tallness from the tall parent and a factor for shortness from the short parent. But all the offspring are tall since the tallness factor is dominant over the shortness factor (which is known as recessive). Recessive factors can become dominant when two occur in a single individual, as in short plants of the second generation.

↑ Gregor Mendel's experiments with pea plants laid the foundations for the modern science of genetics.

Timeline

1856 Mendel begins experiments with pea plants

1865 Mendel reports to Brünn Natural History Society

1866 Mendel publishes his results

1900 De Vries, Correns and Tschermak–Seysenegg confirm Mendel's findings

---

1843 The world's first underwater tunnel is completed beneath the Thames in London.

1844 US dentist Horace Wells uses nitrous oxide ('laughing gas') as an anaesthetic.

1845 German zoologist Karl Siebold shows that protozoa are single-celled organisms.

1843　　　　1844　　　　1845

1842 African-American inventor Norbert Rillieux designs a vacuum evaporator for extracting juice from sugarcane.

1844 US inventor Samuel Morse sends the first message by telegraph in the United States.

1845 French physicists take detailed photographs of the Sun.

Tortoiseshell Cats

Genes for black and ginger pigments are carried on the X chromosome. Black (B) is dominant over ginger (b). Females have two X chromosomes, so they can be black (BB), ginger (bb) or tortoiseshell (Bb). Males have only one X (and one Y), so they can only be black (B) or ginger (b). Males can not be tortoiseshell – which needs one black (B) and one ginger (b) allele – because they have only one X chromosome.

➤ This diagram shows how tortoiseshell cats get their mixture of black and ginger colours.

Mendel proposed two laws. The law of segregation states that the two factors controlling each hereditary characteristic segregate and pass into separate germ cells (egg and sperm). The law of independent assortment states that the pairs of factors segregate independently of each other during the formation of germ cells. He reported his results in 1865, publishing them a year later, but nobody took much notice at the time.

Building on Mendel's Work

Mendel's 'factors' are now called alleles, which are alternative forms of a gene. There are two alleles of each gene in any cell, one inherited from each parent, which occupy the same place on a chromosome. Usually one allele is dominant, and the other is recessive. A germ cell (gamete) – egg or sperm – has one allele. When egg and sperm combine at fertilisation, the

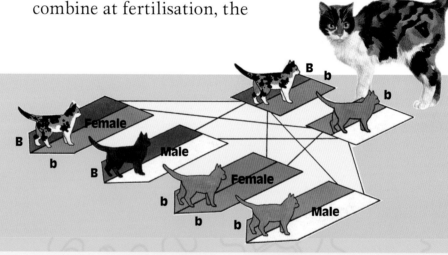

TIMELINE
1845–1850

KEY:

- Astronomy and Maths
- Chemistry and Physics
- Biology and Medicine
- Inventions and Engineering

1845   1846   1847

1845 German physicist Franz Neumann publishes his theory of electromagnetic induction.

1846 US inventor Elias Howe invents a lock-stitch sewing machine.

1846 German astronomer Johann Galle is the first person to observe the planet Neptune.

1845 British engineer Isambard Brunel launches the first successful propeller-driven ship, SS *Great Britain*.

1846 The Smithsonian Institution is founded in Washington, DC.

1847 The American Medical Association is founded in Philadelphia.

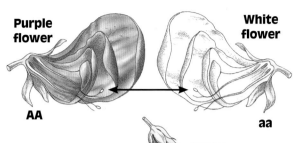

Purple flower

White flower

AA

aa

→ Pea plants grow quickly, so Mendel was easily able to check his predictions.

two alleles come together in a new individual that inherits characteristics from each parent. The appearance of the new individual depends on which of these characteristics (if any) is dominant.

After Mendel's death, several biologists independently studied inheritance in plants. In Holland, Hugo de Vries came up with identical results to Mendel's, which he announced in 1900. This led to German botanist Karl Correns and Austrian botanist Erich von Tschermak-Seysenegg publishing their observations, which confirmed Mendel had been right.

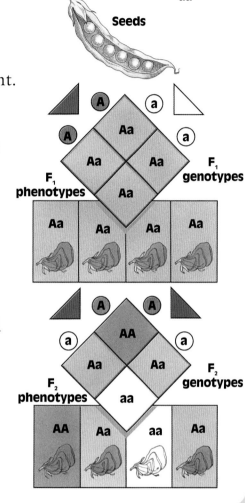

Seeds

F_1 phenotypes

F_1 genotypes

F_2 phenotypes

F_2 genotypes

Predicting Colours of Pea Plants

This diagram shows how Mendel's laws allow us to predict the colours that will be produced by crossing purple-flowered pea plants with white-flowered pea plants. Purple is dominant, and the first generation (known as F1 phenotypes) produced by planting seeds from the cross are all purple. But when this first generation is interbred in turn, the second generation (known as F2 phenotypes) has purple or white flowers in the ratio 3 purple to 1 white.

1848 Scottish physicist William Thomson, Lord Kelvin, introduces the absolute temperature (or Kelvin) scale.

1849 Swiss embryologist Rudolf von Kölliker states that nerve endings are extensions of nerve cells.

1848

1849

1850

1848 US inventor James Bogardus introduces a method of making cast-iron buildings.

1849 Anglo-American engineer James Francis makes an improved reaction water turbine.

1850 English physician Alfred Higginson invents the hypodermic needle, initially for extracting samples of blood.

The Periodic Table

By 1869, following many new discoveries, there were 63 known chemical elements. From these, Dmitri Mendeleyev constructed his famous periodic table.

← Mendeleyev's periodic table later provided an insight into atomic structure.

TIMELINE
1850–1855

KEY:

- Astronomy and Maths
- Chemistry and Physics
- Biology and Medicine
- Inventions and Engineering

ca 1850 German chemist Robert Bunsen begins using the Bunsen burner.

1851 French physicist Léon Foucault constructs Foucault's pendulum and uses it to prove the rotation of Earth.

1852 US inventor Elisha Otis patents the safety lift.

1850

1851

1852

1850 German physicist Rudolf Clausius formulates the second law of thermodynamics. It states that heat will not on its own move from a hot object to a hotter one.

1851 US inventor Isaac Singer makes a single-thread sewing machine.

Russian chemist Dmitri Mendeleyev (1834–1907) was born in Tobolsk, Siberia, the youngest child of a large middle-class family. Despite the death of his father when Dmitri was 13, his mother was determined her youngest son should receive good schooling. He won a place at the Pedagogical Institute in St Petersburg, a centre for teacher training, qualifying as a teacher in 1855. He later studied chemistry at the University of St Petersburg and in Germany. He took up a university post at St Petersburg, and in 1869 began writing a textbook on chemistry (in those days inorganic chemistry).

Making the Table

Wishing to find order in the jumble of elements, he wrote the name of each on a card. He then dealt sets of 'hands', like dealing out playing cards. He arranged the elements in order of increasing atomic weight (the average mass of an atom of the element). Mendeleyev saw that if he started a new row of cards with every eighth element, those elements with similar chemical properties fell one above the other in columns.

↓ Mendeleyev's work laid the foundations for all modern chemistry.

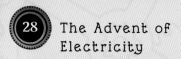

The Modern Periodic Table

Today's periodic table contains about 50 more elements than in Mendeleyev's time. They are arranged in order of their atomic numbers in seven horizontal 'periods' of varying length. Two long series of 14 elements each – the lanthanides and the actinides – are shown in separate lines on page 29. The system of using a letter or letters to denote the symbol for each element (for example, Fe = iron) was introduced by Swedish chemist Jöns Berzelius (1779–1848) in 1818.

Mendeleyev saw that properties tended to recur along each row – there was a 'periodicity' in the properties. He named his new grid of rows and columns the periodic table. He even included in the table additional 'missing' elements that were still to be discovered. He predicted the chemical and physical properties of these elements, their atomic weights and melting points.

In 1875, French chemist Paul Lecoq de Boisbaudran discovered 'eka-aluminium' (in a space below aluminium), naming it gallium; in 1879, Swedish chemist Lars Nilson discovered 'eka-boron' (below boron) and named it scandium; and in 1886, German chemist Clemens Winkler discovered 'eka-silicon' (below silicon) and named it germanium. Mendeleyev's predictions had been fulfilled. By 1914, only seven gaps in the table remained up to element 92.

Atomic Structure

The atomic number is the total number of protons in an atom of any element. The modern periodic table is better described as being arranged in order of atomic number. Chemists have introduced the term 'neutron number' (number of neutrons in the atom's nucleus) and call atomic weights 'relative atomic masses'.

Mendeleyev could not explain the reason for the periodicity of the elements. That had to await an understanding of the structure of atoms, particularly

TIMELINE
1855–1860

KEY:

- Astronomy and Maths
- Chemistry and Physics
- Biology and Medicine
- Inventions and Engineering

1855

1856

1857

1855 Italian physicist Luigi Palmieri designs a seismograph for measuring earthquakes.

1856 Remains of Neanderthal people are discovered by workers in Germany.

1856 English steelmaker Henry Bessemer develops the Bessemer converter for making steel out of iron.

1855 English physicist John Pratt shows that gravity remains constant everywhere at sea level.

1856 English chemist William Perkin invents mauveine, the first synthetic dye, which becomes the basis of a huge industry.

1857 French chemist Louis Pasteur observes that microorganisms cause fermentation.

how electrons arrange themselves around the nucleus of an atom. In the 20th century, chemists realised that the periodic table reflected the atomic structures of the elements as electrons fill up shells surrounding the nucleus. The periodic table enables chemists to predict more accurately what reactions are possible. In 1955, Mendeleyev received the ultimate honour when the element 101 was named mendelevium.

↓ Mendeleyev left gaps in the periodic table where he thought that elements would fit: all those gaps have now been filled. New elements have also been added to the table.

1	2	3	4	5	6	7	8	9	10	11	12	13	14	15	16	17	18
1 H 1.0079																	2 He 4.0026
3 Li 6.941	4 Be 9.0122											5 B 10.811	6 C 12.011	7 N 14.0067	8 O 15.9994	9 F 18.9984	10 Ne 20.1797
11 Na 22.9898	12 Mg 24.3050											13 Al 26.9815	14 Si 28.0855	15 P 30.9738	16 S 32.066	17 Cl 35.4527	18 Ar 39.948
19 K 39.0983	20 Ca 40.078	21 Sc 44.9559	22 Ti 47.88	23 V 50.9415	24 Cr 51.9961	25 Mn 54.9380	26 Fe 55.847	27 Co 58.9332	28 Ni 58.6934	29 Cu 63.546	30 Zn 65.39	31 Ga 69.723	32 Ge 72.61	33 As 74.9216	34 Se 78.96	35 Br 79.904	36 Kr 83.80
37 Rb 85.4678	38 Sr 87.62	39 Y 88.9058	40 Zr 91.224	41 Nb 92.9064	42 Mo 95.94	43 Tc 98.9072	44 Ru 101.07	45 Rh 102.9055	46 Pd 106.42	47 Ag 107.8682	48 Cd 112.411	49 In 114.82	50 Sn 118.710	51 Sb 121.76	52 Te 121.757	53 I 126.0945	54 Xe 131.29
55 Cs 132.9054	56 Ba 137.327	57 La 138.9055	72 Hf 178.49	73 Ta 180.9479	74 W 183.85	75 Re 186.207	76 Os 190.2	77 Ir 192.22	78 Pt 195.08	79 Au 196.9665	80 Hg 200.59	81 Tl 204.3833	82 Pb 207.2	83 Bi 208.9804	84 Po 208.9824	85 At 209.9871	86 Rn 222.0176
87 Fr 223.0197	88 Ra 226.0254	89 Ac 227.0278	104 Rf 261.11	105 Db 262.114	106 Sg 263.118	107 Bh 262.12	108 Hs (265)	109 Mt (266)	110 Uun (269)	111 Uuu (272)	112 Uub (277)		114 Uuq (285)		116 Uuh (289)		118 Uuo (293)

Lanthanide series:

58 Ce 140.115	59 Pr 140.9076	60 Nd 144.24	61 Pm 144.9127	62 Sm 150.36	63 Eu 151.965	64 Gd 157.25	65 Tb 158.9253	66 Dy 162.50	67 Ho 164.9303	68 Er 167.26	69 Tm 168.9342	70 Yb 173.04	71 Lu 174.967

Actinide series:

90 Th 222.0381	91 Pa 223.0359	92 U 238.0289	93 Np 237.0482	94 Pu 244.0642	95 Am 243.0614	96 Cm 247.0703	97 Bk 247.0703	98 Cf 251.0796	99 Es 252.083	100 Fm 257.0951	101 Md 258.10	102 No 259.1009	103 Lr 262.11

Atomic number — 29
Chemical symbol of element — Cu
Atomic weight — 63.546

1858 English anatomist Henry Gray publishes his famous book, *Anatomy of the Human Body*, or *Gray's Anatomy*.

1859 Charles Darwin publishes *On the Origin of Species*, the book in which he puts forward his theory of evolution.

1858 1859 1860

1858 The first transatlantic submarine telegraph cable is laid.

1859 The world's first productive oil well is drilled in Pennsylvania by Edwin Drake.

1859 German chemist Hermann Kolbe synthesises salicylic acid, leading to the mass production of the first synthetic drug, aspirin.

Germs and Disease

During the middle of the 19th century, scientists finally realised that germs cause most diseases and no longer blamed 'evil spirits' or 'bad air'.

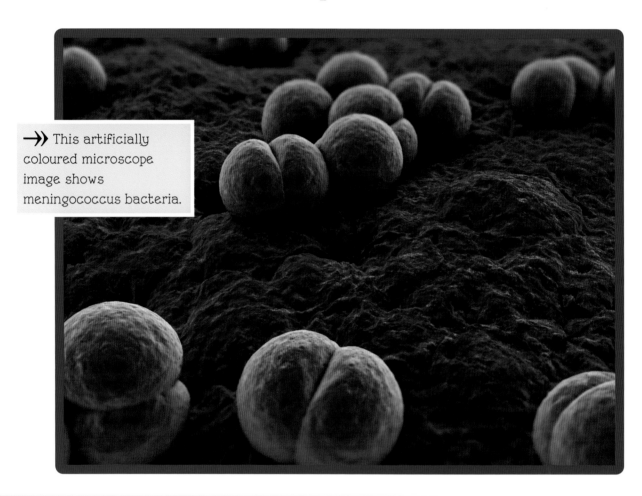

➤➤ This artificially coloured microscope image shows meningococcus bacteria.

TIMELINE
1860–1865

KEY:

- Astronomy and Maths
- Chemistry and Physics
- Biology and Medicine
- Inventions and Engineering

1860 German scientists Robert Bunsen and Gustav Kirchhoff develop a method of analysing substances by their spectra.

1861 In Australia, the first large-scale food-freezing plant is built to prepare meat for export to Britain.

1862 Swedish astronomer Anders Angström uses a spectroscope to identify hydrogen in the Sun's atmosphere.

1860

1861

1862

1860 English nurse Florence Nightingale sets up the first training school for nurses, in London.

1861 English physicist William Crookes uses spectrography to identify the element thallium.

1862 US gunsmith Richard Gatling patents a 10-barrel machine gun.

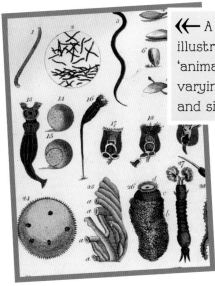

← A 19th-century illustration shows 'animacules' of varying shapes and sizes.

As early as 1546, Italian physician Girolamo Fracastoro suggested in *On Contagion and Contagious Diseases* that germs are the cause of disease. Nobody took much notice, even after 1676, when Dutch scientist Antonie van Leeuwenhoek first saw bacteria, using a homemade microscope. The bacteria were from his own mouth and were probably not disease-carrying.

Germ Theory of Disease

Then, in 1840, German pathologist Jacob Henle put forward the idea that infection is caused by parasitic organisms, the so-called germ theory of disease, which was later proposed independently by French chemist Louis Pasteur. In 1877, German bacteriologist Robert Koch announced that bacteria could be stained to make them easier to study under a microscope. Seven years later, Danish physician Hans Gram extended this idea as a means of classifying bacteria, which since then have been dubbed either Gram-positive or Gram-negative

Timeline

1546 Fracastoro suggests germs cause disease

1676 Van Leeuwenhoek discovers bacteria

1840 Henle's germ theory of disease

1884 Gram's stain is used to classify bacteria

1897 Beijerinck discovers the existence of viruses

↓ Antonie van Leeuwenhoek used this microscope to observe bacteria.

1863 French chemist Louis Pasteur introduces pasteurisation, a process that kills bacteria in food and drink.

1863 The world's first underground railway, the Metropolitan Line, opens in London.

1863   1864   1865

1863 Swedish chemist Alfred Nobel begins experimenting with the explosive nitroglycerin.

1864 Scottish physicist James Clerk Maxwell publishes Maxwell's equations, which describe mathematically electromagnetic phenomena.

1864 French engineer Pierre Michaux makes the first pedal bicycle.

Viruses

Viruses evaded discovery until the late 19th century. They turned out to have various shapes and to consist of an outer 'container' of protein holding a molecule of DNA (deoxyribonucleic acid) or RNA (ribonucleic acid). They cannot multiply outside a living cell; but once they force their way into a cell, they make it rapidly produce more virus particles that break out and invade other cells.

⟹ Shown here are: an adenovirus (A); a bacteriophage (B); and HIV (human immunodeficiency virus).

depending on their capacity to absorb a special stain. Bacteriologists also classify bacteria according to their shapes: coccus (round), bacillus (oval), spirochete (spiral) and so on.

Once biologists knew what bacteria looked like, the hunt was on. Scientists who handled cultures of infectious diseases often put themselves at great risk, but results came quickly. In 1880, German bacteriologist Karl Eberth found the bacillus that causes typhoid. In 1882, fellow German Robert Koch found the bacterium that causes tuberculosis, while German researchers also identified

⬆ Louis Pasteur used rabbits and other animals in his studies of bacteria.

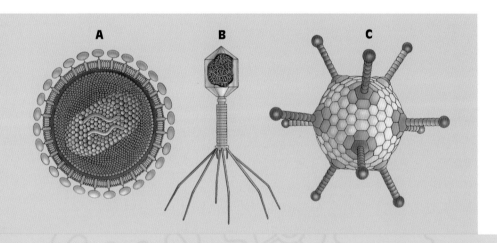

A   B   C

TIMELINE
1865–1870

KEY:

- Astronomy and Maths
- Chemistry and Physics
- Biology and Medicine
- Inventions and Engineering

1865 Austrian monk Gregor Mendel formulates his laws of inheritance.

1865 Belgian chemist Jean Servais Stas devises the first modern tables of atomic weights using oxygen as a standard.

1867 Swedish chemist Alfred Nobel patents dynamite in Britain.

1865   1866   1867

1865 US locksmith Linus Yale perfects the cylinder lock and receives a second patent for it.

1866 Italian astronomer Giovanni Schiaparelli shows that meteor showers are associated with the orbits of comets.

1867 English surgeon Joseph Lister introduces carbolic acid (phenol) as a disinfectant in hospital.

the cause of the animal disease glanders. In 1897, Danish veterinarian Bernhard Bang discovered a bacillus that causes abortion in cattle and the Japanese Kiyoshi Shiga found the cause of the disease endemic dysentery.

Other Microorganisms

Bacteria are not the only parasitic microorganisms to cause human diseases. Protozoans, for example, include the trypanosomes that cause sleeping sickness and Chagas disease, the amoebas that result in amoebic dysentery and the *Plasmodium* parasite responsible for malaria. Some microscopic fungi produce diseases that affect the skin or lungs. Most of these microorganisms were tracked down by 19th-century microbiologists.

In 1897, Dutch microbiologist Martinus Beijerinck proved that the microorganism that causes tobacco mosaic disease escapes through a filter that traps bacteria. He had discovered the first virus. Since then, viruses have been found to be responsible for many diseases in humans, including yellow fever, influenza, polio, measles and AIDS (acquired immune deficiency syndrome). Almost as fast as bacteriologists found bacteria, they developed vaccines against them, so that people could be injected and gain immunity. Vaccines for virus diseases proved more difficult, but now exist for all the disorders named above except AIDS.

⬆ The German Robert Koch discovered the bacterium that causes tuberculosis. His breakthrough was the first step in finding a cure for one of the biggest killers of the 19th century.

1868 US engineer George Westinghouse designs the air brake for steam locomotives.

1869 Swiss pathologist Johann Miescher isolates deoxyribonucleic acid (DNA), which he calls 'nuclein'.

1869 The Suez Canal between the Mediterranean and Red Sea in Egypt is built by French engineer Ferdinand de Lesseps.

1868   1869   1870

1868 English astronomer William Huggins observes that the star Sirius is receding from Earth.

1869 Russian chemist Dmitri Mendeleyev compiles the first periodic table of the elements.

1869 The first transcontinental railway, the Union Pacific, is completed in the United States.

The Internal Combustion Engine

In the steam engines that powered the Industrial Revolution, external combustion took place. But the internal combustion engine is much more efficient.

→→ German inventor Karl Benz and his assistant ride on an 1885 Benz Motorwagen.

TIMELINE
1870–1875

KEY:

- Astronomy and Maths
- Chemistry and Physics
- Biology and Medicine
- Inventions and Engineering

1870 German chemist Rudolf Fittig makes aromatic hydrocarbons by combining two molecules of a halogen compound in the presence of sodium metal.

1871 German chemist Felix Hoppe-Seyler discovers invertase, the first enzyme to be isolated.

1872 German mathematician Richard Dedekind publishes his theory of irrational numbers.

1870

1871

1872

1870 German physicist Ernst Abbe introduces the use of his condenser to provide illumination for microscopes.

1871 US engineer Simon Ingersoll invents a pneumatic rock drill.

1871 English inventor James Starley patents the 'penny-farthing' bicycle.

The Belgian engineer Étienne Lenoir made the first successful engine to burn fuel internally in 1859. It ran on coal gas, which was mixed with air and sucked into the cylinder by the movement of a piston. It generated about 745 watts (1 horsepower) and worked in two jerky stages with the help of a heavy flywheel.

The First Engines

In 1862, French engineer Alphonse Beau de Rochas patented an engine that worked in four stages, or strokes. He did not build an actual engine, and the idea was later taken up by a self-taught German engineer, Nikolaus Otto. In 1876, Otto made his first horizontal four-stroke gas engine; it produced 2.2 kilowatts (3 horsepower). The four-stroke cycle is still the basis of today's modern engines.

Otto's engine still used coal gas. In 1867, the Austrian engineer Siegfried Marcus invented a carburettor that vaporised liquid petrol and mixed it with air. Two German engineers, Karl Benz and Gottlieb Daimler, independently made the first petrol-burning internal combustion engines in 1885. Both engines were used to develop motor vehicles. Daimler's engine ran at 900 revolutions per minute

Timeline

1859 Lenoir makes the first gas-burning engine

1876 Otto manufactures the four-stroke gas engine

1885 Benz and Daimler create the gasoline engine

1892 Rudolf Diesel invents the engine named after him

⬆ This German stamp celebrates Rudolf Diesel, who invented the diesel engine in 1892.

1873 French engineer Amédée Bollée constructs a steam-powered car.

1874 US physician Andrew Still founds osteopathy, which uses manipulation of bones and joints to treat diseases.

1875 A safe loading level for ships, called the Plimsoll line, is introduced in Britain, and soon taken up everywhere.

1873   1874   1875

1873 Scottish physicist James Clerk Maxwell publishes his electromagnetic theory of light: that light is a form of electromagnetic radiation (like radio waves and X-rays).

1874 Irish physicist George Stoney coins the phrase 'electrine' for the fundamental unit of electricity; later he changes it to 'electron'.

The Two-stroke Engine

In a two-stroke engine, the piston acts as a valve. On the upstroke, the piston compresses the fuel-and-air mixture, which is ignited by a spark from the spark plug. The piston closes off the exhaust port. The explosion forces the piston down, the downstroke. Exhaust gases escape via the uncovered port, and as the piston rises again, fresh fuel-and-air is sucked in through the open inlet port.

⟩⟩ The up-and-down motion of the piston is turned into rotary motion by a crankshaft.

(rpm) and used a red-hot platinum tube to ignite the fuel and a carburettor that had been invented by his business partner, German engineer Wilhelm Maybach. The engine built by Benz was slower than Daimler's and produced less than 745 watts (1 horsepower), but the car he used it in had many modern features, including coil ignition powered by a battery and a distributor.

Improving Engines

By the end of the 19th century, the scientific principle of engines was being analysed. If a suitable fuel–air mixture is hot and compressed enough, it will combust spontaneously. The Englishman Herbert Stuart patented the first example of a compression-ignition engine in 1890. Two years later, a German inventor, Rudolf Diesel, patented a similar engine; he demonstrated it in 1897. Since then, this type of engine has been known as a diesel engine.

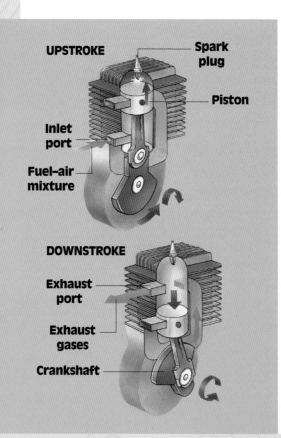

UPSTROKE — Spark plug
— Piston
Inlet port
Fuel–air mixture

DOWNSTROKE
Exhaust port
Exhaust gases
Crankshaft

TIMELINE
1875–1880

KEY:
- Astronomy and Maths
- Chemistry and Physics
- Biology and Medicine
- Inventions and Engineering

1875

1875 French physicist Jules Violle measures the solar constant – the amount of the Sun's energy that reaches the top of Earth's atmosphere.

1876

1876 German botanist Eduard Strasburger describes mitosis, the process of cell division into two identical cells.

1877 German bacteriologist Robert Koch develops a way of staining bacteria to make them easier to study.

1877

1876 Scottish-born US engineer Alexander Graham Bell patents the telephone.

1876 US librarian Melvil Dewey introduces the Dewey Decimal System for cataloguing library books.

1876 German engineer Nikolaus Otto builds a four-stroke internal combustion engine fuelled by coal gas.

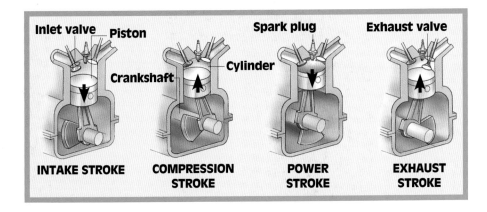

Inlet valve — Piston — Spark plug — Exhaust valve — Crankshaft — Cylinder

INTAKE STROKE — COMPRESSION STROKE — POWER STROKE — EXHAUST STROKE

↑ This diagram shows the four strokes of a standard four-stroke engine.

A diesel engine has several advantages. It uses a less refined, and therefore cheaper, fuel than petrol. The engine needs no spark plugs or associated ignition system and is 35 per cent efficient in fuel consumption, compared with 25 per cent for the best petrol engines. Both figures are far off the theoretical maximum efficiency of 67 per cent for a perfect heat engine.

The early petrol (and all diesel) engines were examples of reciprocating engines. There were some 'rotary' petrol engines, developed very successfully to power propeller-driven aircraft.

In 1929, German engineer Felix Wankel patented a revolutionary internal combustion engine that was truly rotary. The first prototype was made in 1956. A Wankel engine has a rotor that rotates inside a 'cylinder' shaped like a fat figure of eight.

The Four-stroke Engine

In a four-stroke engine, on the intake stroke, the inlet valve opens as the piston moves down. This sucks a fuel-and-air mixture into the cylinder. On the compression stroke, the inlet valve closes and the piston rises, compressing the fuel and air. During the power stroke, the spark plug ignites the fuel, which explodes, and the hot gases force the piston down. On the fourth stroke, the exhaust valve opens to allow gases to escape while the piston rises.

1878 US inventor Thomas Alva Edison demonstrates his electric lightbulb.

1879 English inventor Henry Lawson invents the 'safety' bicycle, driven by a chain to the rear wheel – the model for all modern bicycles.

1878

1879

1880

1878 US astronomer Asaph Hall discovers the two moons of Mars, Phobos and Deimos.

1879 US chemists discover saccharin, an artificial sweetener 2,000 times sweeter than sugar.

1880 French chemist Louis Pasteur identifies the *Streptococcus* bacterium.

Sources of Electricity

Before 1800, scientists knew only about static electricity – a positive or negative charge on an object – but then an Italian physicist produced a moving electric current.

→ Volta shows off his battery, or voltaic pile, to Napoleon I, the emperor of France.

In 1791, Italian physician Luigi Galvani reported what he called 'animal electricity'. Dissecting a dead frog, he found the animal's muscles twitched when he touched them with two different metals. In 1800, Count Alessandro Volta, an Italian physicist, replaced the animal tissue with a cardboard disc soaked in salt solution. He put a piece of copper or silver on one side and zinc on the other side. Wires connected to the metal plates carried an electric current. Volta found he could obtain higher voltages by making a stack of such discs

TIMELINE 1880–1885

1880 Scottish astronomer George Forbes predicts the existence of 'Planet X' orbiting beyond Neptune: Pluto is discovered in 1930.

1881 US astronomer Henry Draper takes the first photographs of comets.

1882 German bacteriologist Robert Koch discovers the bacterium that causes tuberculosis and, in 1883, the one that causes cholera.

KEY:

- Astronomy and Maths
- Chemistry and Physics
- Biology and Medicine
- Inventions and Engineering

1880   1881   1882

1880 German bacteriologist Karl Eberth discovers the bacterium that causes typhoid fever.

1881 English physicist J.J. Thomson predicts that an object's mass changes when it becomes electrically charged.

1882 The first US steam-powered electricity-generating station opens in New York City.

to form a voltaic battery (the first true battery). Today, scientists call such a battery a primary cell. The pieces of metal are electrodes, and the solution between them is an electrolyte.

In 1836, English chemist John Daniell produced a more efficient primary cell. Its current was steadier than that of Volta's cell and overcame the problem of polarisation – a build-up of hydrogen bubbles that eventually causes the voltaic pile to stop working.

Volta's Successors

The Leclanché cell, a battery invented in 1866 by French engineer Georges Leclanché, also avoids polarisation. It uses an electrolyte of ammonium chloride solution. It produces about 1.5 volts. Today's common type of dry battery has the same system.

The German chemist Robert Bunsen made a zinc–carbon primary cell; using acid electrolytes, it produces 1.9 volts. The cadmium cell, invented in 1893 by English-born American electrical engineer Edward Weston, produces

Timeline

1800 Alessandro Volta invents the voltaic pile

1836 John Daniell introduces his primary cell

1866 Georges Leclanché invents the Leclanché cell

1872 The Clark standard cell is introduced, using zinc

1893 Edward Weston invents the cadmium cell

1900 Thomas Edison invents the nickel–iron accumulator

⬸ Luigi Galvani discovered that a frog's limbs twitched if he applied two types of metal to create an electric charge.

1884 US-born English inventor Hiram Maxim makes the first fully automatic machine gun.

1884 US engineer Frank Sprague – 'the father of electric railway traction' – forms the Sprague Electric Railway and Motor Company.

1883   1884   1885

1883 Belgian engineer Étienne Lenoir invents the spark plug (for internal combustion engines).

1884 German physiologist Max Rubner shows that the body makes use of carbohydrates, fats and proteins in order to produce energy.

1884 German astronomer Max Wolf discover's Wolf's comet, which takes seven years to orbit the Sun.

The Primary Cell Battery

A primary cell, such as the dry battery for a torch (below right), can be used only until its chemicals run out, when it has to be thrown away (carefully). In this type of cell, the electrolyte is a paste of ammonium chloride and gum. The zinc cathode forms the case of the battery, and manganese dioxide and carbon surround the central carbon anode.

→→ This battery uses carbon and zinc for the anode and cathode, respectively.

1.0186 volts, and in 1908 the scientific community accepted it as a standard of voltage. It is known as the Weston standard cell. English electrical engineer Josiah Clark invented the Clark standard cell 21 years earlier, in 1872, using zinc instead of cadmium.

A primary cell stops working when it is fully discharged. A secondary cell (or storage cell, or accumulator) can be recharged. In 1859, French chemist Gaston Planté devised the lead–acid accumulator. It is the earliest and most commonly used battery, used in most cars. It has one electrode (or 'plate') of lead and one of lead covered with lead oxide, which dip into a sulphuric acid electrolyte. Another type, the alkaline nickel–iron accumulator, or Ni–Fe cell, was invented in 1900 by American inventor Thomas Edison.

⬆ The Leclanché cell used the same principles as most modern dry batteries.

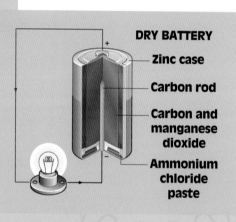

DRY BATTERY

- Zinc case
- Carbon rod
- Carbon and manganese dioxide
- Ammonium chloride paste

TIMELINE
1885–1890

KEY:
- Astronomy and Maths
- Chemistry and Physics
- Biology and Medicine
- Inventions and Engineering

1885   1886   1887

1885 Austrian doctor Sigmund Freud develops psychoanalysis as a diagnostic procedure.

1885 French chemist Louis Pasteur produces a vaccine against rabies.

1887 German physicist Heinrich Hertz detects radio waves.

1885 US architect William Jenney builds the world's first skyscraper, a steel-framed building in Chicago.

1885 US electrical engineer William Stanley invents the transformer.

1886 US chemist John Pemberton invents Coca-Cola.

When any accumulator becomes discharged, it can be connected to a supply of DC (direct current) and recharged. For example, as a car's motor is running, the battery is continually recharged.

Both primary and secondary cells convert chemical energy into electrical energy. In doing so, they 'consume' materials in the electrodes or electrolyte. A fuel cell, however, converts the chemical energy of a fuel directly into electrical energy. The first fuel cell, which 'consumed' hydrogen and oxygen gases, was demonstrated in 1839 by Welsh physicist and judge William Grove.

Volta is the best-remembered scientist. He gave his name to the volt, adopted in 1905 as the SI unit of electric potential.

↓ Car batteries are secondary cells, or accumulators, that are charged by the engine.

Secondary Cell

A secondary cell, or accumulator, can be recharged. It has lead and lead-oxide electrodes in a sulphuric acid electrolyte. In use, sulphate ions react with the lead cathode to produce lead sulphate and release electrons. To recharge the accumulator, current from an outside source is passed through the battery in the opposite direction. This reverses the reactions at the electrodes, re-forming lead and lead oxide. The accumulator is then ready for use again.

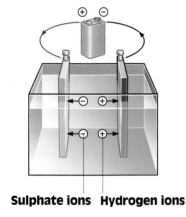

ACCUMULATOR ON CHARGE

Sulphate ions   Hydrogen ions

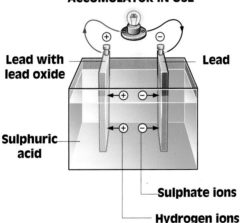

ACCUMULATOR IN USE

Lead with lead oxide

Lead

Sulphuric acid

Sulphate ions

Hydrogen ions

1889 Swedish physical chemist Svante Arrhenius derives the Arrhenius equation, a way of calculating the speed of a chemical reaction.

1889 US astronomer Edward Barnard takes the first photographs of the Milky Way (our galaxy).

1888   1889   1890

1888 Danish astronomer Johan Dreyer publishes a new catalogue of nebulae and star clusters.

1889 The Eiffel Tower is completed in Paris, France.

1890 US inventor Herman Hollerith invents a punch-card reader (for recording census results).

The Elusive Electron

Today, every science student knows the importance of an electron in understanding electricity and atomic physics. A century ago, things were very different.

↑ English physicist J. J. Thomson experimented with cathode rays.

TIMELINE
1890–1895

KEY:

Astronomy and Maths

Chemistry and Physics

Biology and Medicine

Inventions and Engineering

1890 German bacteriologists produce antitoxins against the diseases diphtheria and tetanus.

1891 German engineer Otto Lilienthal makes a steerable human-carrying glider.

1892 English scientist Francis Galton argues that no two people have the same fingerprints, and that fingerprints can be used in crime investigation.

1890

1891

1892

1890 Russian physiologist Ivan Pavlov experiments with dogs to study how nerve impulses stimulate digestive secretion in the stomach.

1892 German bacteriologist Robert Koch introduces filtration of water to control a cholera epidemic in Hamburg, Germany.

Until the end of the 19th century, discoveries in physics had left unanswered questions such as: objects can hold a charge of static electricity, but what form does the charge take? What are the electric current charges that flow along a conductor and are they different from the electrostatic ones? A high voltage across the plates of a vacuum tube produces cathode rays, but what are the rays made of? And if matter is made of atoms, what are atoms made of?

The First Answers

The answer to these questions came from one invention – the vacuum pump. Scientists could now remove most of the air from any apparatus. Around 1850, the German laboratory equipment manufacturer Heinrich Geissler sealed metal plates inside a glass vacuum tube containing traces of a gas. He connected the plates to a source of high-voltage electricity and obtained pretty lighting effects as the gas glowed.

Geissler tubes were used by two German physicists: Julius Plücker in 1859 and Johann

Timeline

Timeline

1850 Geissler tubes invented

1874 Stoney predicts existence of electrons

1879 Crookes suggests cathode rays are particles

1891 Stoney names the electron

1895 Perrin shows cathode rays are negative charges

1897 Electron discovered

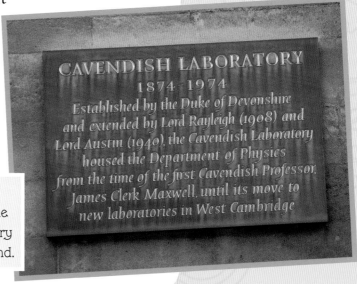

CAVENDISH LABORATORY
1874-1974
Established by the Duke of Devonshire and extended by Lord Rayleigh (1908) and Lord Austin (1919), the Cavendish Laboratory housed the Department of Physics from the time of the first Cavendish Professor, James Clerk Maxwell, until its move to new laboratories in West Cambridge

→ This plaque marks the site of the Cavendish Laboratory in Cambridge, England.

1893 African-American surgeon Daniel Williams performs the first open-heart surgery.

1893 The French Lumière brothers invent a motion-picture camera.

1895 Swedish and Scottish chemists independently discover helium on Earth (previously it was only known in the Sun's spectrum).

1893

1894

1895

1893 German engineer Rudolf Diesel first builds a compression-ignition engine (diesel engine).

1894 US astronomer Percival Lowell sets up a private observatory at Flagstaff, Arizona, to search for the ninth planet.

1895 German physicist Wilhelm Röntgen takes the first X-ray.

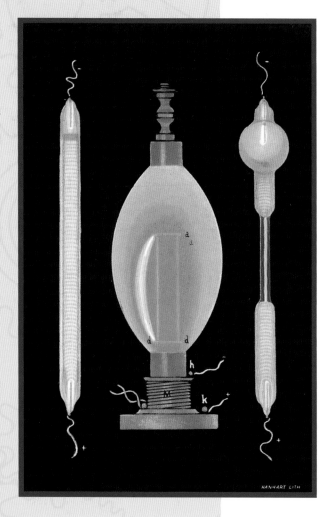

Geissler tubes are glass tubes or bulbs with most of the air pumped out of them.

Hittorf in 1869. They claimed the light resulted from 'rays' travelling in the Geissler tube. In 1879, English physicist William Crookes suggested the 'rays' might be particles. Sixteen years later, French physicist Jean Perrin showed they were negatively charged.

Thomson and Cathode Rays

Then along came the English physicist J. J. Thomson. At age 14, he trained as a railway engineer, then won a scholarship to Cambridge University, graduating in 1880. He worked in the Cavendish Laboratory, and became head of the laboratory in 1884.

Thomson deflected cathode rays with electric and magnetic fields, measured their speed (proving they travel more slowly than light waves), and worked out the ratio of their charge (e) to their mass (m). Thomson deduced that cathode rays must consist of minute negatively charged particles. He announced the discovery of the first subatomic particles in 1897, and in 1899 found they have a mass equal to about one two-thousandth of the mass of a hydrogen atom. In 1874, George Stoney had predicted their existence. In 1891, Stoney named them 'electrons'. The electron was the unit of electricity responsible for electrostatic charges. It

TIMELINE
1895–1900

KEY:

- Astronomy and Maths
- Chemistry and Physics
- Biology and Medicine
- Inventions and Engineering

1895

1896

1897

1896 French physicist Henri Becquerel discovers radioactivity.

1896 New Zealand-born British physicist Ernest Rutherford describes and names alpha particles (which are helium nuclei) and beta particles (which are electrons).

1895 US inventor King Gillette has the idea for the disposable double-edge razor blade.

1897 German physicist Ferdinand Braun invents the cathode-ray tube, later used in radar and TV sets.

1897 English physicist J.J. Thomson identifies the electron, the first subatomic particle.

This diagram shows three types of electrical flow through a cable.

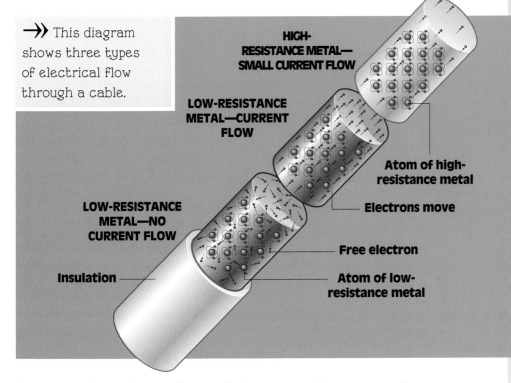

HIGH-RESISTANCE METAL—SMALL CURRENT FLOW

LOW-RESISTANCE METAL—CURRENT FLOW

Atom of high-resistance metal

Electrons move

LOW-RESISTANCE METAL—NO CURRENT FLOW

Free electron

Insulation

Atom of low-resistance metal

Electricity Flow

Electrons occur in all atoms. In most metals – such as the copper in electric cable – many electrons leave their atoms to form a 'sea' of free electrons (bottom of diagram). When a voltage is applied (middle section), the free electrons move to form an electric current. Copper is said to have low resistance. A metal with high resistance, such as tungsten used in electric heaters, has few free electrons (top section). A voltage causes only a small current and the metal becomes hot.

became clear that a flow of electrons along a conductor was an electric current. Since electrons come from the metal of the cathode, they must be part of all atoms.

Thomson studied positive rays, which led in 1912 to a way of separating charged particles. In 1919, the English physicist Francis Aston created the mass spectrograph. When Thomson retired in 1919, he was succeeded by his former assistant, Ernest Rutherford. Rutherford eventually proposed a structure for the atom that included the atomic nucleus. Seven of Thomson's assistants won Nobel prizes. He received it in 1906.

1898 English physician Ronald Ross finds the microorganism *Plasmodium*, which causes malaria, in the stomach of a mosquito; he argues that mosquito bites transfer the parasite to humans.

1900 Austrian-born US pathologist Karl Landsteiner discovers the A, B and O blood groups and their intercompatibility.

1898

1899

1900

1898 French chemists Marie and Pierre Curie discover the elements polonium and radium.

1898 English physiologist John Langley identifies the autonomic nervous system, which controls involuntary muscles and glands.

1900 German physicist Max Planck proposes the quantum theory: that radiation is emitted in separate 'packets', or quanta.

Glossary

absolute zero The lowest temperature possible (equal to −273.15°C/−459.67°F).

ammonite A fossil of an ancient sea mollusc.

aromatic hydrocarbons A class of compounds containing a benzene ring.

atom The smallest unit that matter can be divided into and still retain its chemical identity.

bacteria (singular bacterium) Microscopic organisms that can cause disease.

carbonised Converted to carbon by heat.

chromosome A thread-like structure in the nucleus of a living cell that carries the genetic information.

capacitance Ability to store an electric charge.

compound, chemical A substance in which molecules are made up from atoms of more than one element.

conductor Any substance that allows an electric current, heat or sound to pass through it.

ecology The study of the relationship of plants and animals to their environment and to each other.

electric current A flow of electrons through a conductor.

electromagnetism The phenomenon by which magnetic fields can be produced by the flow of electrons in an electrical current.

electron A negatively charged subatomic particle.

element Any substance that cannot be split chemically into simpler substances.

gene The basic unit of inheritance that controls a characteristic of an organism.

geology The group of sciences concerned with the study of Earth, including its structure, long-term history, composition and origins.

invertebrate An animal lacking a backbone.

ion An atom or molecule with an electric charge.

microorganism The general term for any living organism that is invisible to the naked eye but visible under a microscope.

mollusc A type of invertebrate that usually has an external shell.

nebula A cloud of dust and gas in outer space.

neutron A subatomic particle with no electric charge.

petrified Turned into a stony substance.

photosynthesis The process by which green plants convert light energy from the Sun.

plankton Microscopic organisms floating in water.

proton A subatomic particle with a positive electrical charge.

sedimentary rock Rock formed from layers of deposited sediment.

SI Abbreviation for the International System of units.

spectrography The study of chemical radiation.

spectroscope A device for observing the spectra of light or radiation.

subatomic particle Any particle that is smaller than an atom.

thermostat A device that automatically regulates temperature.

vaccine A preparation containing viruses or other microorganisms introduced into the body to build up immunity against infectious disease.

virus A tiny parasitic organism that can reproduce only inside the cell of its host.

zooplankton Plankton made up of small animals and the immature stages of larger animals.

Further Reading

Books

Arbuthnot, Gill. *A Beginner's Guide to the Periodic Table.* A & C Black, 2014.

Christensen, Clarence. *Ernest Rutherford: 170 Success Facts* (All You Need to Know). Emereo Publishing, 2014.

Ganeri, Anita. *Michael Faraday* (What Would You Ask?). Belitha Press, 2000.

Morton, Alan. *Splitting the Atom* (Milestones in Modern Science). Evans Brothers, 2008.

Oxlade, Chris. *Nuclear Energy* (Tales of Invention). Raintree, 2012.

Winston, Robert. *Evolution Revolution: From Darwin to DNA.* Dorling Kindersley, 2009.

Wood, A. J., and Clint Twist. *Charles Darwin and the Beagle Adventure.* Templar Books, 2009.

Websites

http://inventors.about.com/cs/ inventorsalphabet/a/electricity.htm
About.com's page on the discovery of electricity, with many links.

www.periodicvideos.com/
The University of Nottingham's interactive videos of the periodic table.

www.amnh.org/exhibitions/ darwin/
The American Museum of Natural History's pages on Darwin's life and work.

www.dnaftb.org/1/index.html
Pages about Gregor Mendel with an animation of his genetic experiments.

www.bbc.co.uk/history/historic_ figures/rutherford_ernest.shtml
BBC History biography of Ernest Rutherford.

Index